HONESTY
IS THE BEST
IMAGE
Tom Wilson

...THE HIGH POINT OF MY LIFE WAS FEBRUARY 20TH, 1977, WHEN I HIT NINE GREEN LIGHTS IN A ROW !!
Tom Wilson

ZIGGY®'S PLACE

Andrews, McMeel & Parker
A Universal Press Syndicate Company
Kansas City • New York

ZIGGY® is syndicated internationally by Universal Press Syndicate.

 For information write Andrews, McMeel & Parker, a Universal Press Syndicate Company, 4400 Johnson Drive, Fairway, Kansas 66205.

ISBN: 0-8362-7961-1

Library of Congress Catalog Card Number: 84-73473

SPECIAL
CHEF'S
SURPRISE
TOM WILSON

THE
LADDER
OF
SUCCESS
Tom Wilson

GRIN
BEAR IT
tom wilson

PHARMACY
HERE'S YOUR PRESCRIPTION !!
TOM WILSON

SOON TO BE A MAJOR GOVERNMENT SPENDING PROGRAM
Tom Wilson

RETURNS
LOOK AT THE SIGN !! ...DOES IT SAY ANYTHING ABOUT "REFUNDS"?
Tom Wilson

YOU WEIGH 147 POUNDS, AND YOUR FLY IS OPEN.
TOM WILSON

...MAY i HAVE THE SEED CATALOG WHEN YOU'RE DONE WITH iT...?
TOM WILSON

MOST DOGS WANT TO GO FOR WALKS !!
Tom Wilson

TEST YOUR
SALES RESISTANCE
50¢
Tom Wilson

SHOPPING MALL
INFORMATION

... WHERE DID I PARK MY CAR?
Tom Wilson

PLEASE HELP
STILL ONLY 25¢
Tom Wilson

PLEASE
DO NOT
FEED THE
PIGEONS
POP
CORN
Tom Wilson

SURE, I'LL ITEMIZE...
EIGHT DOLLARS FOR THE VISIT... 29¢ FOR THE BANDAGE AND $53.75 FOR THE MALPRACTICE INSURANCE!
TOM WILSON

SORRY...THIS LINE IS FOR EIGHT ITEMS OR LESS, AND YOU'VE GOT A DOZEN EGGS THERE!
EGGS
Tom Wilson

IT'S TEN O'CLOCK... DO YOU KNOW WHERE THE BANK IS KEEPING YOUR MONEY ?
Tom Wilson

the WRONG BUS
BUS STOP
Tom Wilson

...WE WERE GOING TO MAKE AN EXAMPLE OF YOU, MR. ZIGGY, BUT THEN WE FIGURED THAT ANYONE WHO SUPPORTS A DUCK, A CAT, A DOG, A FISH, A PARROT, AND A CARTOONIST DESERVES A BREAK!
I.R.S.

Tom Wilson

THANK YOU FOR OBEYING THIS SIGN !!
Tom Wilson

I'LL CHECK THE CARBURETOR FIRST,...IT'S USUALLY THE CARBURETOR WITH THESE CREAM-COLORED CARS!

Tom Wilson

ED'S
ALL-YOU-CAN-EAT DINE
PIG IN
PIG OUT
TOM WILSON

...LAST NIGHT I FOUND AN OMEN IN MY ALPHABET SOUP !!
Tom Wilson

...IT IS A SMALL CAR, BUT THE PAYMENTS WILL GIVE YOU THAT BIG CAR FEELING !!

Tom Wilson

I CHECK THE COIN RETURNS OF PAY PHONES....WHAT DO YOU DO FOR A LIVING?
Tom Wilson

YES, THIS FORTUNE-TELLING BUSINESS IS PRETTY GOOD THESE DAYS, BUT.... WHO KNOWS WHAT TOMORROW WILL BRING !!
Tom Wilson

I'M AN AVERAGE AMERICAN ...BRING ME 3½ CUPS OF COFFEE!

Tom Wilson

TO MAKE A LONG STORY SHORT
..WHATEVER YOU'RE DOING,
STOP IT !!

Tom Wilson

YOU WILL BE HUNGRY AGAIN IN ONE HOUR
Chungs

...MY PROBLEM IS THAT I LIKE THINGS AS THEY AREN'T !!
Tom Wilson

INSURAN
HERE'S YOUR POLICY, SIR...
...AND HEY!...LET'S BE
CAREFUL OUT THERE, OKAY?!!
Tom Wilson

GREETING CARDS
GET WELL
GET SERIOUS
SHAPE UP
GET OFF IT
COME OFF IT!
Tom Wilson

...THANKS, BUT i HAVEN'T FiNiSHED MY OLD SET YET!
ENCYCLOPEDIAS
Tom Wilson

... SAME TIME TOMORROW, OKAY?
Tom Wilson

PLEASE STAND BY...
...I HAVE TEMPORARILY LOST OUR TV DINNERS!
Tom Wilson

...CONGRATULATIONS...YOU ARE MY 10,000TH CUSTOMER...
I'M KNOCKING A FREE 15 POUNDS OFF YOUR WEIGHT!!
TOM WILSON

..THAT'S THE NEWS... NOW HERE'S "BUTTERCUP" WITH THE FARM REPORT..
TOM WILSON

WOW! TALK ABOUT NIGHTMARES ...I SAW MY LIFE PASS BEFORE MY EYES... AND I WASN'T IN IT!!
TomWilson

137 DAYS WITHOUT GOING BANANAS
Tom Wilson

THIS IS
THE SQUIRREL LIBERATION FRONTÉ
YOUR
PARK
Tom Wilson

WELL, AFTER ALL, SIR...
YOU KNEW THIS MEAL COULD BE DANGEROUS WHEN YOU ORDERED IT!
Tom Wilson

Designer Sunglasses
... I'M SORRY, SIR... YOU JUST DON'T HAVE A DESIGNER FACE !!
Tom Wilson

STUCK IN THE SIXTIES
PLEASE HELP

SAUSAGE, PEPPERONI AND BLACK OLIVES...THAT MAKES THREE WISHES!!

Tom Wilson

AMALGAMATED INC.
...AND IF YOU DO WELL, ZIGGY...WE'LL SEE ABOUT GETTING YOU A COMPANY CAR !!
SALES KIT
Tom Wilson

Till 14 MAR '86!

...ANOTHER PATIENT WITH ACUTE DEPRESSION ?...
WHY ME ?!!
Tom Wilson

HI!...I'M THE BLUEBIRD OF IMMEDIATE GRATIFICATION!
Tom Wilson

CARRIES NO CASH
Tom Wilson

POLITICAL CAMPAIGNING NEXT 2,500 MILES
Tom Wilson

...I'M SORRY, BUT I DON'T KNOW "MUSKRAT RAMBLE"!
TOM WILSON

...YOUR PROBLEM IS LOW SELF-ESTEEM ...IT'S VERY COMMON AMONG LOSERS!!
Tom Wilson

CUTE!

IT'S THE LATEST THING....
GENERIC MONOGRAMS !!
WHAT'S-HIS-NAME
Tom Wilson

MILLSTONE
&
SONS
NEPOTISTS
Tom Wilson

GOOD DAY, SIR, I REPRESENT THE "I WAS AFRAID SOMETHING LIKE THIS WAS GOING TO HAPPEN" INSURANCE COMPANY...

TOM WILSON

BOOKS
BEST SELLER
SOON TO BE A MAJOR SLANDER TRIAL!!
TomWilson

...OF COURSE IT'S OUT OF STYLE, BEING OUT OF STYLE IS THE LATEST THING !!
TomWilson

...I'M WATCHING, I'M WATCHING!!
TOM WILSON

GUINNESS BOOK OF PEOPLE WHO DON'T EVEN TRY!
Tom Wilson

HI! YOUR REGULAR REFLECTION COULDN'T MAKE IT THIS MORNING!

Tom Wilson

PIECE-O-PIZZA
...A PIZZA WITH EVERYTHING. ONLY I WANT THE ANCHOVIES ON THE SIDE.
Tom Wilson

CAUTION
MEN
RETIRED
tom wilson

PSSST, BUDDY!
YOU GOT THE TIME?
TOM WILSON

THE HUMAN BODY IS THE LORD'S TEMPLE, MR. ZIGGY, BUT YOURS IS IN SERIOUS DANGER OF BEING TORN DOWN TO MAKE WAY FOR A PARKING LOT !!
tom wilson

YOU'LL NEVER TAKE ME ALIVE !! ...IF YOU WANT ME, YOU'RE GONNA HAFTA COME IN AND GET ME, COPPER !!
Tom Wilson

...YOU REALIZE I'M GOING TO HAVE TO CHARGE YOU DOUBLE!!
Tom Wilson

PUSH BUTTON TO KILL TIME
Tom Wilson

YOUR WEIGHT
AND
MISFORTUNE
1¢
Tom Wilson

OPTOMETRIST
DON'T WORRY.... NOBODY'S EYES CAN KEEP UP WITH THOSE LITTLE NUMBERS ON THE GAS PUMPS ANYMORE !!
A
EB
GF
HID
UR
Tom Wilson

OFFICIAL
PANHANDLER
OF THE
1984
OLYMPICS

...PERHAPS YOU'D BE INTERESTED IN OUR "TILL HELL FREEZES OVER" PLAN...
MORTGAGES
Tom Wilson

EXPECTED
FEARED

VIDEO GAMES
IT'S OUR BEST SELLER ...AN I.R.S. AGENT CHASES YOU THROUGH THE GALAXY !!
SPACE EVADERS
Tom Wilson

I.R.S.
OVER 10 MILLION AUDITED
Tom Wilson

...I THINK I HAVE A TOUGH TIME MAKING DECISIONS...
OF COURSE, THAT'S FOR YOU TO DECIDE....
Tom Wilson

...DID YOU KNOW THAT YOUR LIPS MOVE WHEN YOU READ?
TOM WILSON

Andre's
SIDEWALK CAFE
...WE'D LIKE A TABLE NEAR A TREE !!
Tom Wilson

LOST AND FOUND
...CAN i JUST LOOK THROUGH YOUR STOReROOM? ...i'Ve LOST HUNDReDS OF THiNGS !!
Tom Wilson

...ARE YOU SURE YOU WANT TO KNOW THE MEANING OF LIFE? ...THERE'S NOTHING YOU CAN DO ABOUT IT ANYWAY!!
Tom Wilson

...TAKE IT FROM ME, YOUNG FELLA... OLD AGE IS NOT FOR SISSIES !!
Tom Wilson

MOTEL
$10.00 A ROOM
BASE RATE
...NOW THEN, WILL YOU BE WANTING ANY FURNITURE?
Tom Wilson

...I FINALLY GOT IN TOUCH WITH MY INNER SELF ...AND IT SAID I SHOULD MIND MY OWN BUSINESS!
TomWilson

...WELL, SOMEBODY ATE THE SESAME SEEDS OFF MY HAMBURGER BUN!
Tom Wilson

CAN'T YOU DO YOUR CALISTHENICS SOME OTHER TIME?
PEOPLE
Tom Wilson

POP
Tom Wilson

...I KNOW YOU ORDERED A HAMBURGER, BUT LIVER IS BETTER FOR YOU !!

MOM'S DINER

Tom Wilson

THIS CONCLUDES OUR PROGRAMMING DAY ...GOOD LUCK OUT THERE IN THE REAL WORLD!!
tom wilson

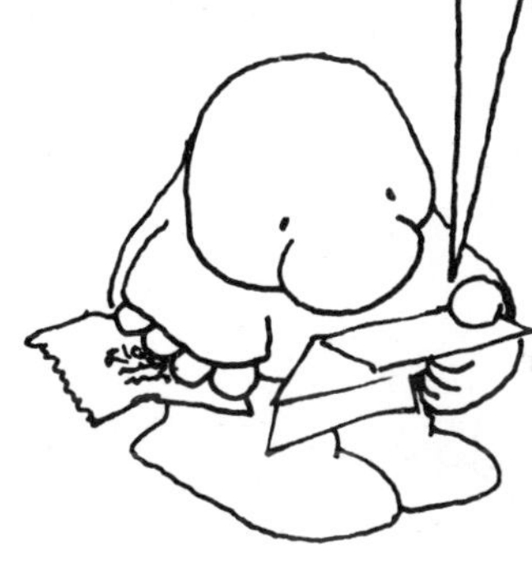
~ CONGRATULATIONS ~
YOU HAVE BEEN VOTED
"SUCKER OF THE YEAR"
PLEASE SEND $100.00 TO
HAVE YOUR AWARD ENGRAVED!
Tom Wilson

OF COURSE THERE'S NO COLOR ....WE'RE IN A BLACK-AND-WHITE NEWSPAPER CARTOON !!
T.V. REPAIR
Tom Wilson

PHONES
$5.00
AND UP
Tom Wilson

...WE'LL HAVE YOU UP AND AROUND IN NO TIME... YOUR INSURANCE RUNS OUT THURSDAY!!

Tom Wilson

IN
OUT
PIG OUT
CHIPS
CHOCOLATE CHIP COOKIES
COLA
TOM WILSON

...BEFORE I BRING YOU THE TOMATO SURPRISE, SIR... YOU HAVE TO PROMISE NOT TO REVEAL THE ENDING !!
Tom Wilson

OBEDIENCE SCHOOL
...HE DIDN'T MAKE THE FETCHING TEAM!
Tom Wilson

...ON MY EGO TRIPS i TRAVEL TOURiST !!
Tom Wilson

...THERE'S NOT MUCH I CAN DO AT THIS POINT... BRING HIM BACK AFTER HE HATCHES!
VET
Tom Wilson

INFORMATION
...WHY CAN'T i DO ANYTHING RIGHT?
Tom Wilson

...i DON'T THINK i LIKE THE BREAKUP... NOW i'VE GOT SEVEN DIFFERENT PHONE COMPANIES REACHING OUT AND TOUCHING ME!
Tom Wilson

...YOU'VE GOT A BAD CASE OF HYPOCHONDRIA....
I'M TAKING YOU OFF "AFTER M*A*S*H,"
"ST. ELSEWHERE," AND "TRAPPER JOHN."

Tom Wilson

GET SPRUNG WITH SPRINGER
J.P. SPRINGER ATTORNEY AT LAW
...i LIKED iT BETTER WHEN THEY COULDN'T ADVERTISE!
Tom Wilson

SCHOOL OF
HARD KNOCKS
KNOCK
HARD
Tom Wilson

TO ERR IS HUMAN
..WHO PUT THAT THERE?
Tom Wilson

ONE OF MANY WAYS
Tom Wilson

GROWING UP CONSISTS OF A VARIETY OF SUBSTITUTES FOR YOUR THUMB!
Tom Wilson

...WHAT WE HAVE HERE IS A FAILURE TO COMMUNICATE !!
Tom Wilson

IN
OUT
Tom Wilson

...I STARTED OUT AS A CHARACTER IN A NOVEL... BUT I COULDN'T REMEMBER MY LINES... SO I BECAME A CARTOON CHARACTER !!

Tom Wilson

SLIPPERS
50¢
Tom Wilson

...i KNOW THE AD SAID NO SALESMAN WOULD CALL ... BUT i'M REALLY NOT MUCH OF A SALESMAN!
TOM WILSON

...I DON'T HAVE ANY 'CAUSE I'VE NEVER STAYED AT ANY HOTEL WHOSE NAME STARTS WITH THE LETTER Z !!
Tom Wilson

Mother Hubbard's
RESTAURANT
...THERE'LL BE A SLIGHT DELAY, SIR ...THE DISH RAN AWAY WITH THE SPOON !!
wilson

OF COURSE IT'S YOU, SIR ... IT'S ANYBODY!
Tom Wilson

... AND EVER SINCE I FOUND OUT THAT BABE RUTH STRUCK OUT 1,330 TIMES.... I'VE BEEN FEELING LOTS BETTER!!
Tom Wilson

IF YOU DON'T SEE WHAT YOU WANT ... LOWER YOUR EXPECTATIONS
Tom Wilson

HUMAN
DIGNITY
SOLD
OUT
Tom Wilson

BANK MONEY MACHINE
INSERT CARD HERE
...NEVER MIND WHAT i WANT iT FOR !!
Tom Wilson

JUST LOOK AT THIS PHONE BILL !! WILL YOU COOL IT WITH THE CALL-IN SHOWS ?
Tom Wilson

...IT'S A TYPICAL CASE OF DEPRESSION... I'M GIVING YOU A PRESCRIPTION FOR SOME ROSE-COLORED GLASSES!!
Tom Wilson

INFORMATION
...WHAT DID i EVER DO TO DESERVE THIS?
Tom Wilson

...i'M NOT MAD! i JUST WANT TO KNOW HOW YOU GOT iT iN THERE!!

ONE OF THE GOOD THINGS ABOUT SLEEPING IS... YOU CAN'T EAT WHILE YOU'RE SLEEPING !!

GOOD ONE!

...THEY KEEP RUNNING THE SAME XEROX COMMERCIAL OVER AND OVER AND OVER...,
Tom Wilson

...WELL! YOU CERTAINLY MADE A FOOL OUT OF YOURSELF LAST NIGHT!
Tom Wilson

Tom Wilson

...I'VE BEEN THROUGH COLIC, ADOLESCENCE, PUBERTY, AND THE TERRIBLE TEENS
...NOW IF YOU CAN JUST GET ME THROUGH THIS WEEK'S EPISODES OF "GENERAL HOSPITAL," I'LL HAVE IT MADE !!
Tom Wilson

...FOR SOME REASON, EVEN MY SUMMER DOLDRUMS AREN'T AS EXCITING AS THEY USED TO BE !!
Tom Wilson

...IT ISN'T REALLY NECESSARY TO SMILE FOR AN X-RAY !!
Tom Wilson

...THIS YEAR, EVERYTHING'S COMING UP ROSES ...BUT I PLANTED BROCCOLI !!
Tom Wilson

...WHENEVER I HEAR A VOICE IN THE WILDERNESS ...IT'S ALWAYS YELLING "TIMBER!"

...IF YOU PLAY GOLF, STOP!!
IF YOU DON'T, START!!
Tom Wilson

...MY IDENTITY CRISIS STARTED
DURING THE "ME" GENERATION.

Tom Wilson

BOOKS
...IT'S THE STORY OF AN EPIC STRUGGLE BETWEEN MAN AND COMPUTER !!
MOBY DISK
Tom Wilson

JOE'S BAR
UNDER NEW JOE!
Tom Wilson

GO AWAY... WE WON'T BE RIGHT BACK !!
TOM WILSON

TUNNEL OF
MEANINGFUL
RELATIONSHIPS

THAT'S A NICE LITTLE GARDEN YOU'VE GOT THERE ... HOW'D YOU LIKE TO MAKE SURE NOTHING HAPPENS TO IT?!
Tom Wilson

I'M NOT COMPLAINING... I JUST NEVER HAD "JELL-O FLAMBÉ" BEFORE !!
Tom Wilson

NEEDS NO
INTRODUCTION
Tom Wilson

...IT'S NOT MUCH, BUT IT'S ONLY THREE MINUTES TO DOWNTOWN !!
Tom Wilson

GAS
FREE
SALAD BAR
WITH EACH
FILL-UP!
Tom Wilson

MOM'S DINER
SPEAK WHEN YOU'RE SPOKEN TO
MOM'S
Tom Wilson

...IT'S NOT SUPPOSED TO GROW LEAVES, SIR ...WHAT YOU HAVE HERE IS A TELEPHONE POLE!
TREE SURGEON
Tom Wilson

GIBBONS
EXTERMINATORS
WE MAKE
MOUSE CALLS
Tom Wilson

COURT HOUSE
TRIALS
TRIBULATIONS
TOM WILSON

EDGAR Q. ?
? — 1984
"HE DRANK
TO FORGET"
Tom Wilson

BIG RALPH'S DINER
TODAY'S SPECIAL
KNUCKLE SANDWICH
Tom Wilson

INFORMATION
...AM i COMING OR GOiNG ?
Tom Wilson

FORGOT WHERE
i BURIED MY
NUTS
PLEASE HELP
Tom Wilson

THINGS TO DO TODAY
1. FORGET YOUR TROUBLES
2. COME ON
3. GET HAPPY
Tom Wilson

...DO YOU REALLY LIKE CRACKERS, OR IS IT JUST AN ETHNIC THING ?
Tom Wilson

...AND REMEMBER, WE WOULDN'T PROGRAM GARBAGE LIKE THIS IF PEOPLE LIKE YOU DIDN'T WATCH IT ALL THE TIME!
TOM WILSON

CLEANERS
"NO JOB IS TOO BIG
OR TOO SMALL"
...IT ISN'T TOO BIG
OR TOO SMALL...
IT'S TOO DIRTY!!
Tom Wilson

...MY MOST EMBARRASSING MOMENT?
...I BREAK THE RECORD EVERY DAY!
Tom Wilson

...THIS IS GOING TO BE A TRICKY DIAGNOSIS....
PICK A NUMBER BETWEEN ONE AND TEN !!

Tom Wilson

TODAY'S OCEAN SOUNDS HAVE BEEN BROUGHT TO YOU BY ATLANTIC RICHFIELD!
Tom Wilson

PHOBIA BOOKSTORE
FEAR OF FLYING
FEAR OF DRIVING
FEAR OF WALKING
FEAR OF STAYING AT HOME
Tom Wilson

ENTERING
TOWNVILLE
A GENERIC
COMMUNITY
TOM WILSON

SMALL
TALK
50¢
tomwilson

EFFICIENCY
EXPERT
OUT TO
LUNCH
BACK IN
4MIN. 18SEC.
Tom Wilson

T.V. DINNERS
PARENTAL DISCRETION ADVISED
TOM WILSON

MOM'S DINER
...THE FOOD IS GREAT...BUT I'M NOT REALLY CRAZY ABOUT THE CHAIRS!
MENU
Tom Wilson

JOE'S BAR
HAPPY HOUR
4:00-5:00 P.M.
WE RESERVE THE RIGHT TO REFUSE HAPPINESS TO ANYONE.
Tom Wilson

NOW, YOU JUST DO AS I'VE TOLD YOU, AND I'M SURE THAT OLD INFERIORITY COMPLEX WILL BE GONE IN NO TIME!!
Tom Wilson

COPS
'R'
US
Tom Wilson

AND NOW IN RESPONSE TO ALL YOUR REQUESTS, WE PRESENT.... "CHAINSAW ROLLER DERBY."
TOM WILSON

YOU MAY ALREADY HAVE WON!
YOUR MATCHING NUMBER IS
43193124610745331786552789
31415926801072523589826466
14553692681437630981537219
29746305174954822079572136
ZIGGY
Tom Wilson

HOLD STILL... I THINK YOU'VE GOT THE BUG THAT'S BEEN GOING AROUND.
Tom Wilson

THOUGHT FOR TODAY

TRY NOT TO THINK ABOUT IT !!

THE TROUBLE IS NOT WITH YOUR SET...

TRAUMATIZED
BY EVENTS
PLEASE
HELP
TomWilson

...I HATE TO TELL YOU THIS, BUT SO FAR TODAY YOU'VE BEEN CONTRADICTED BY A WEIGHT-AND-FORTUNE MACHINE, A NEWSPAPER HOROSCOPE, AND A FORTUNE COOKIE!!
Tom Wilson

KILROY WAS MUGGED HERE!
TOM WILSON

THAT WAS IT!
...THERE IS
NO NEXT
EXIT
tom wilson

...THE GOOD HUMOR MAN DEPRESSES ME!
Tom Wilson

WELL ...IF YOU DON'T WANT TO MEET SOME GIRLS...WOULD YOU BE INTERESTED IN SOME ALUMINUM SIDING...?
TAXI

UPCREEK AIRLINES
....SORRY, SIR....BUT OUR "NO CLASS" SECTION IS FILLED!
Tom Wilson

HMMMMMM....VERY ODD...
YOUR PILOT LIGHT SEEMS
TO HAVE GONE OUT !!
Tom Wilson

...WELL...NO NEWS IS GOOD NEWS !!
Tom Wilson

LOOK... YOU CAN'T SOLVE ALL YOUR PROBLEMS BY ROLLING OVER AND PLAYING DEAD!
Tom Wilson

ASK A SILLY QUESTION
50¢
Tom Wilson

NOW...THIS ONE WAS OWNED BY A LITTLE OLD LADY.... NOTICE THE NICE SLIPCOVER!
Tom Wilson

HILL ST.
LET'S BE CAREFUL
Tom Wilson

IT'S DEPRESSION....
STOP LETTING HIM WATCH
THOSE DOG-AND-CAT
CARTOONS ON TV.
Tom Wilson

NO, THANKS.... WHEN I WANT TO KNOW SOMETHING, I JUST WRITE TO DEAR ABBY!
ENCYCLOPEDIAS
TOM WILSON

OCT 31
BOO
OCT 30
Tom Wilson

FIX-IT
SHOP
THROW-IT-AWAY-
AND-BUY-
ANOTHER-ONE-
SHOP
Tom Wilson

... MIND IF I USE YOUR OUTLET TO CHARGE MY ELECTRIC CAR?
Tom Wilson

HE FOLLOWED ME HOME, AND WANTS TO KNOW IF HE CAN KEEP ME!
Tom Wilson

..NOW, THIS BABY IS LOADED WITH EXTRAS!
Tom Wilson

TUNNEL
OF
LOVE
NO KINKY STUFF
Tom Wilson

...MARSHMALLOW IS THE ONLY FOOD THAT TASTES GOOD EVEN WHEN IT'S COOKED WRONG!

FURRIER
FURRIEST
Tom Wilson

CHANTER,
WASCO,
HAMMEREN,
GONSER,
WALKER and
ROBERTSON
Great Ideas that
Just might work!
Tom Wilson

...I ASKED HIM FOR A BALLPARK ESTIMATE, ...AND HE NAMED REGGIE JACKSON'S SALARY!!
Tom Wilson

AN
ENCOURAGING
WORD 50¢
Tom Wilson

...I'LL WAIT A COUPLE OF DAYS TO SEND YOU YOUR BILL...

...I DON'T WANT YOU GNASHING THOSE TEETH FOR A WHILE!

NAMEM
BLAMEM
SHAMEM
AND
FRAMEM
ATTORNEY$
AT LAW
Tom Wilson

...He WITHDREW FROM HIS C.D. EARLY!
TELLER
Tom Wilson

DRIVE THE NEW 1984 GARFIELD
...i GUESS iT WAS ONLY A MATTER OF TiME...
TOM WiLSON

... IT HAD TO HAPPEN SOONER OR LATER... A BUNCH OF WIVES ARE TEARING DOWN THE GOALPOSTS BEFORE THE GAME !!
Tom Wilson

...YOU SHOULD HAVE "GONE POTTY" <u>BEFORE</u> THE SESSION !!

Tom Wilson

...I DON'T MIND THE FARMING, IT KINDA TICKLES, BUT THE STRIP MINING HURTS!!

2-2

Tom Wilson

STRANGEST CASE I'VE EVER SEEN
..., EVEN WITH THE SET UNPLUGGED,
YOU'RE STILL PICKING UP
FOOTBALL !!

Tom Wilson

THIS IS JOHN GIBBONS SUBSTITUTING FOR BOB JAMES, WHO CAN'T FIND HIS HAIR SPRAY!!
Tom Wilson

OVERQUALIFIED
AND
WAITING FOR
TECHNOLOGY
TO CATCH UP!
TOM WILSON

LIFE IS A GAME ...BUT YOU MUST BE PRESENT TO WIN !!

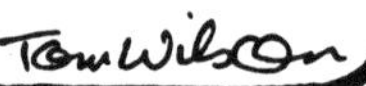

IMPEACH BIG BROTHER!
...IT'S NOT EXACTLY LIKE ORWELL PICTURED IT !!
Tom Wilson

OFFICIAL BATHROOM TISSUE
OF THE 1984 OLYMPICS
Tom Wilson

COMING SOON
SPRING
Tom Wilson

...HAVE YOU EVER WONDERED WHY I NEVER CALLED YOU "FUZZ, THE WONDER DOG"?!
TOM WILSON

Gino's
HOTE
...THIS PLACE LOOKS A LITTLE RICH FOR MY BLOOD !!
GENTLEMEN MUST WEAR GUCCIS
Tom Wilson

PSYCHIATRIST
...WHILE YOU'RE WAITING TO SEE THE DOCTOR, WOULD YOU LIKE TO SEE SOME "LOONEY TUNES"?
TOM WILSON

MENSWEAR
...HERE'S YOUR JOHNNY CARSON SLACKS, SIR.... AND A FREE BOOKLET OF "HOW COLD WAS IT?" JOKES !!
Tom Wilson

I.R.S.
AUDIT
INSURANCE
$5.00

...I COULDN'T FIND A SINGLE THING WRONG WITH YOUR RETURN, MR. ZIGGY.

...WHAT ARE YOU UP TO ?!!

I.R.S.

Tom Wilson

LOU & ETHEL'S PHONE BOOTH
...i SUPPOSE THIS WAS TO BE EXPECTED, ONCE THEY BROKE UP THE PHONE COMPANY.
Tom Wilson

...SORRY ABOUT YOUR FORTUNE, BUT YOU KNOW... "GARBAGE IN, GARBAGE OUT !!"
Tom Wilson

INFORMATION
WHERE'S THE BEEF?
Tom Wilson

THE OPINIONS EXPRESSED DURING THIS POLITICAL DEBATE ARE NOT NECESSARILY THOSE OF THE SPEAKERS !!
Tom Wilson

...BECAUSE BONELESS PIGS ARE VERY HARD TO RAISE !!
HAMS $3.95
BONELESS HAMS $18.98
Tom Wilson

INFORMATION
...WHAT HAPPENED TO MICHAEL JACKSON'S OTHER GLOVE?
Tom Wilson

MEN'S SHOP
... IF YOU PAY CASH, YOU ALSO GET THIS FREE BOOK OF 100 SNAPPY COMEBACKS !!
Tom Wilson

... i DON'T HAVE TIME TO TAKE YOU TO THE BEACH TODAY, BUT HERE'S A DOLLAR FOR THE CAR WASH!
Tom Wilson

...BECAUSE LAUGHTER IS THE BEST MEDICINE !!
Tom Wilson

HOLD IT ! THE CHEF LOST HIS CONTACT LENS !!
Tom Wilson

...MY DiARY iS FULL OF DiTTO MARKS!
TOM WILSON

LIBRARY
SHUT UP
(FORMERLY SILENCE)

PETS
....BECAUSE HE KNOWS OVER SEVEN THOUSAND KNOCK-KNOCK JOKES!
$900.00
Tom Wilson

CHILI SPECIAL 10¢
...BECAUSE WE NEED TO EMPTY THE KETTLE BEFORE WE CAN COOK ANYTHING ELSE !!
tom wilson

...i BELIEVE IN SPREADING MY MONEY AROUND IN A LOT OF DIFFERENT BANKS!
Tom Wilson

USED CARS
... BECAUSE i STOLE iT !!
A STEAL AT $1,795.00
tomwilson

..BREADED LIVER, BROCCOLI AND RHUBARB PIE FOR DESSERT ?! ...THAT DOES IT !! I QUIT !!!
TOM WILSON

JOSHY DOESN'T WANT ANOTHER CRACKER.... JOSHY WANTS A GENTLE, EFFECTIVE LAXATIVE!

Tom Wilson

ROBERT G.
DIFORIO
COMPLETE
AND
UNABRIDGED
Tom Wilson

INFORMATION
...THE TROOP SHIP SAILS AT MIDNIGHT TONIGHT!
TOM WILSON

HI, CLONE !!
Tom Wilson

LOANS
COME BACK, SIR! THEY JUST RAISED OUR PRIME INTEREST RATE!!
TOM WILSON

...AND NOW, WELCOME TO "CELEBRITY NAP" WHERE EACH WEEK WE WATCH A FAMOUS PERSONALITY SNOOZE FOR 30 MINUTES!!
Tom Wilson

...IT'S A STRANGE COMBINATION OF GUILT AND PARANOIA.... HE THINKS EVERYBODY IS OUT TO GET HIM, BUT HE ALSO THINKS HE DESERVES IT!
Tom Wilson

THANK YOU
FOR NOT
ENTERING
TOM WILSON

I'LL HAVE TO ASK YOUR AGE, SIR ... WE DON'T GRANT MORTGAGES TO ANYONE FROM THE "ME" GENERATION !!

TELLER

Tom Wilson

...i JUST TOOK A CRASH COURSE in DEFENSIVE DRIVING !!
Tom Wilson

MOM'S DINER
TRESPASSERS WILL BE SPANKED!
tomwilson

...THIS IS SOMEWHAT OF A BASIC OVERSIMPLIFICATION, BUT THE SITUATION IS FUNDAMENTALLY THAT YOU HAVE A LITTLE ANGEL ON YOUR RIGHT SHOULDER AND A LITTLE DEVIL ON YOUR LEFT, AND...
Tom Wilson

WHAT'S THIS NONSENSE ABOUT YOU NOT RENEWING YOUR SUBSCRIPTIONS ?!
TOM WILSON

VETERINARIAN
...NEAR AS I CAN FIGURE, DOC, HE MADE TOO LOW AN APPROACH COMING IN OVER A BADMINTON GAME!
Tom Wilson

...AND AN UNEXPECTED DEVELOPMENT.....
INSPECTOR TWELVE HAS ELOPED WITH THE MAYTAG REPAIRMAN!
TOM WILSON

GOING GETS TOUGH NEXT 45 MILES
TomWilson

...YES, BUT WHO FEEDS HIM?
Tom Wilson

BOOKS
WHEN BAD THINGS HAPPEN TO GOOD PEOPLE
...BUT WHAT ABOUT WHEN GOOD THINGS HAPPEN TO BAD PEOPLE?
Tom Wilson